GOD'S
REPAIR SHOP

Lance Tassi

ISBN 979-8-88685-822-8 (paperback)
ISBN 979-8-88685-823-5 (digital)

Christian Faith Publishing
832 Park Avenue
Meadville, PA 16335
www.christianfaithpublishing.com

Printed in the United States of America

Contents

Introduction

Before you read any of these glorious chapters, all of you need to know just how this book is being brought to you.

It comes directly to us right from God and Jesus Christ. If you have read the writings from my other four books that they have had me to bring your way, then this is already known to you. This once again is their continuation, but it also is being brought to you by the *timing* of both God and Jesus Christ.

The timing for this is also the result of so many thousands of hours that I have conversed with them both for the topics that we will be presenting to all of you. This has taken place over a period of many, many years, and yes, it all still continues. In fact, some of our steadfast conversations for some of these subjects have been going on for over fifty years.

Yes, it would have been nice for me to get all of this to you sooner, but just like it is for everybody else, we always have one thing in common. It is that we are *works in progress*. I'm no more special than any of you in any way at all when it comes to the relationship that I have with them because to them both, they truly love us in the very same way all of the time.

However, in this love, they, for a fact, get to see all of us every day in how much we will love them. Our love for them is not or is never to be a contest, so please do not look for a blue ribbon first prize by loving them. Instead always try extra hard to love them as much as you can. Right to the point of where they both are the most important friends in your life. Period!

This love (or in your wanting of this loving, true relationship) will be an asset in our presentation, but even if you do not want to love them both for whatever the reasons are, then please consider this: It is for sure that these writings will give all of you a better, smarter life.

If you should have an interest in that, then I am sure that you will get the most out of every word that *God's Repair Shop* has to offer.

1

A Great Divide

If you are wondering what this great divide is, then I'll spell it out…
abortion. The very word means the death of a fetus or, in other bold
words, *to kill a developing baby*, and there are no kind words to say it.

The choice for a woman to have an abortion or not has created
a great divide, and no one can deny it. It has even lead to emotional
conversations, loud screaming arguments, and sometimes, this has
even festered into violence, a sad but true statement. The sadder truth
is this: At least 99.9 percent of all abortions never have to happen
at all, *especially in America.* There may be some medical situations
where an abortion could possibly take place or other factors also. I
am not an expert for those situations, and as I've written before, I am
not an expert about God and Jesus Christ (just like nobody on this
Earth is), even if they claim to be one. However, they both advise me
and guide me diligently for the words that they will allow me to put
on paper by the use of a pen and quite a few bottles of Wite-Out.

So please pay attention because the first thing you need to know
are these two very true reasons of why God had Jesus to be born for
all of us. These two reasons are actually self-explanatory, and they are
as follows: to save us from ourselves and to give all of us the graceful
opportunity to become a part of God's very immaculate heaven.

There are surely some other great reasons, but in my truth, I am
also not an expert on all the writings in the Bible. However, think
about His reason to save us from ourselves because every day some
people find ways to kill other people, don't they? As sad as that is,

just think of how many more would be killed if Jesus Christ had not arrived to let us know how wrong that is.

Abortion is not an exception to any way of killing and just think of how extra crazy our crazy world would be if *Jesus Christ had been aborted.* I mean, just think about that because if Jesus were aborted, then nobody could ever get into heaven. As sad and as bad as it is to have so many millions of developing babies to be aborted every year, we also need to think about this. If they were allowed to be born, perhaps all of our lifespans would last even longer.

In the act of killing so many millions of defenseless babies, I have to ask: How many more great doctors, surgeons, chemists, and other of the like could there be among us right now had these abortions not taken place? Some or all of those aborted could have come up with a cure for cancers, heart disease, diabetes, COVID, and so many other things. You can scoff at that sentence if you are pro-abortion, but I don't think that anybody will do that if a doctor tells you or somebody that you truly love. "Sorry! But you only have about two or three months to live because of your stage 4 cancer."

That might be harsh, so I'll be a bit easier by asking, what about all the engineers and like-minded fetuses that have been aborted who could have given us things like cleaner drinking water, cars that could go two hundred miles on a gallon of gas? You know the list can really go on and on to not only make our lives or our Earth to be better but also that we could live a lot healthier lives.

You see, simply put, both God and Jesus Christ do want the very best for all of us, but the only thing stopping us is ourselves. Yes, I know there are fractured governments, societies, churches, and we surely have fractured our Earth. Sadly, too many people sit in a state of denial, permissiveness, or a careless attitude.

To me, at least, if anybody ever thinks that a good way to live or fix what needs fixing up is to start by killing those in a womb instead needs to have a long, spirited conversation with both God and Jesus Christ. I know there sadly are too many who don't believe in them or don't care a lot about anybody else either, but even these kinds of "couldn't care less" thinking people were allowed to be born instead of being aborted. I want them to know, just like those who do believe in my two best friends, that both God and Jesus Christ are right here on this Earth.

My prior books give you that verification, and this new book will give all of you even a lot more of the godly truth information. In fact, they have even allowed specific photographic proof on all of my book covers and more are on my Facebook page. These have also proven just how simple it is that anybody can converse with both of them. However, even if you are a true believer, then how much dedicated time do you give to both of them besides maybe an hour or two on Sunday?

In fact, I just have to ask everybody at least this: What do you ever think that you would have to lose by becoming real best of friends with God and Jesus Christ or to get into a revealing real conversation with them because they both sure can make it to be possible?

This may have taken us away from abortion for a couple of paragraphs, but did it? The godly truth is that life starts in a woman's womb and so do the first spiritual godly adulations. These first heartbeats, if we allow for them to develop, increases everybody's abilities to become better, more humane kinds of people.

We can abort if we choose to, or we can stop almost all of it by the simplest of ways that God and Jesus Christ are going to allow me to present, and you can make all this become a part of your story.

So with that said, we can now put *God's Repair Shop* to be able to fix those acts of abortion, and certainly, God and Jesus will make this to be done with a righteous, commonsense solution.

2

Elimination

To end virtually all abortions by choice, by convenience, or as a way of birth control, we just have to put into place the action of the next two words: *instant adoption*, especially in America. I say America because it is or it was supposed to be a fully developed, true Christian nation. The last book, *The Godly Truth*, went over this in a much greater detail, but I will maintain that no nation can ever be a real true Christian nation if abortions (by the words that God chose in the first sentence of this chapter) are allowed. However, I am not qualified to give any testimony to the abortions that may be needed due to some extenuating circumstances. I am not even close to being a literary scholar, so I'll explain the instant adoption solution way as best as I can.

Instant adoptions simply would allow for anybody over the age of twenty-one to adopt a pregnant woman's baby if she doesn't want it instead of another abortion taking place in the world. Married couples would be preferred, but the ins and outs of who can adopt shouldn't take long to figure out. Other safeguards could also be put into place, and those shouldn't take long to get using some form of standard operating procedure. It should no longer take about fifty thousand dollars or larger sums of money to adopt or take so many years to adopt a child.

A cost of roughly five hundred dollars for the paperwork, etc., should be all that is needed because the lawyers could donate their services (especially if they are Republicans). Also just think of the many thousands of lawyers who are retired who could volunteer to do this, especially if they really want to end as many abortions as possible. Other people could also step in to help them. Empty offices could be rented on the cheap by landlords who want to donate their services to this movement. In fact, I think our US government has millions of square feet of different buildings that they (or we) pay taxes for that just sit empty.

Certainly there are other necessities to organize, but for me to go into all the specifics or research is to be had by others because I really am not smart enough to figure it all out. In fact, I am only on my eighth handwritten page, and I have totally used up a bottle of Wite-Out, all in a good full week of writing. It also takes me about a good year to get a book out to you, and if it wasn't for Linda or Kathy who knows how to type or how to use a computer and whatever else is needed, you wouldn't be reading this. This proves that God and Jesus Christ can make a way for all of us, especially when other lives are on the line.

Together with God and Jesus as our inspiration and our best source of truthful information, let us pray and then join them to have *instant adoption* apply. It truly is a win-win for everybody, and it also is a great victory for us to have with God and Jesus Christ. It will help make both of them to be extra happy and will also lift our spirits in the names of God and Jesus Christ. Let us pray extra hard for the blessings of instant adoption as we still seek an answer to that very question: What would any life be like if Jesus Christ was aborted?

3

War No More

Just so you know, I am not going to bring up all the wars centuries ago or those that historians teach. If we start from the first World War that America fought in and then go on from there, the world lost an extraordinary amount of millions of people; perhaps even over a hundred million or more. I am not a historian, a war buff, or the biggest peacenik that has ever walked the Earth, but I do know that all wars suck. From killing to maiming and to the families of soldiers who get killed, wounded, and even those who make it home, the effects of these wars will stay with them forever.

I am not an expert about war either, but I did have my fill of it by being in the Vietnam War for over a year. Teaching to kill started out right in boot camp, right to the point of systematic hate the enemy and never ever trust anybody who has slanted eyes regardless of their age or be it male or female. I could go into far greater detail, but being in combat zones is not about emotions, excitement, or the entertainment that lots of people experience by what they see on television or some kind of computer game or the war killing games played at arcades.

Real war has blood; limbs coming off bodies that get badly mutilated, and yes, some even vaporize and disappear. If we in America are honest, our propensity for a lot of violence begs us to ask, just how much of a Christian nation are we, and do we make God and Jesus happy with questionable long-lasting wars? Every day, even the warlike killings in our streets or our domestic disputes seem like a war zone as tons of bullets with guns are sold that are needed for protection.

Our politicians seem helpless to stop this, but about every twenty years or so, they put us in a war in one country or another. For sure, we have to protect our country, our allies, and other people throughout the world, but when is enough, enough? Most of our politicians have never been to a war, never even been in the military, and neither have our presidents, yet they talk like they know what they are doing, don't they?

How do we curtail this? How do we know if a war is real, and how do we end the wars that we get into sooner rather than much later? Well, I'll shoot off the cuff with a couple of suggestions, and then I'll go into the conversations that I have had with God and Jesus to have *wars no more* because they both make better things to be possible.

For my first "off the cuff" remark, let's see if our politicians will enact some new laws to help convince us that a war that America is called into action to fight is for our best interest. The first new law would be that all federal, state, city, and yes, even local politicians would have to have their own children between the ages of eighteen and forty-five years old to serve on the front lines for the duration of the war. I mean, the war is either worth it or it's not, and shouldn't our politicians and their families be extra patriotic? Shouldn't they take the lead in whatever actions that they take to protect America?

They could then enact a law saying any company that supplies an American war effort with the goods or services be capped at a 10 percent profit to minimize excessive super great profits. As an example, a bullet that cost them a dollar to make is not purchased by our tax dollars for a hundred times over. They could also make a law that they could not make stock and bond purchases in these companies because I would think they wouldn't want any kind of war blood money to come their way.

Next would start a *list of five*. Simply put, you ask our enemy nations to list the five things they hate about us the most, and then we write out the five things we hate about them. Then together we go to work on this list to see if any significant changes can be made or to give us a chance for better godly solutions. I'm not saying that this will work every time, but doing this has to be better than not trying at all.

I know that we have the United Nations, but I don't know if they keep anything as simple as a list of five or how much they consult with God and Jesus Christ to bring real peace. I'm sure they would tell us that it is more complicated than that. In my opinion, my godly truth is that both God and Jesus Christ didn't put us on Earth to annihilate each other with war. Proof of that is that years ago, they gave somebody the idea to come up with something called the *Peace Corps*. We hear almost nothing about it anymore. So let's expand on that idea, and I'll start with a very revealing statement. All great ideas for peace, for love, and for godly freedom starts out from the spiritual human qualities that God and Jesus Christ want all of us to better ourselves with and killing each other by war after war is really stupid. In fact, even if any person does not believe in that or believe in God along with mighty Jesus, there is one thing that will remain certain. Nobody will ever be able to stop God and Jesus Christ from loving everybody who has ever been aborted or who has lived on this Earth. Yes, they both want everybody to live in real peace.

They both, however, do give us *choices*, and the Peace Corps is, at least to me, a much better idea than war. So why not tap both God and Jesus Christ on their shoulder with more prayer, more faith, and dedicated determination to do the following, at least here in America?

This would be, that for every person in the military, there would also be three to five people in the Peace Corps to do good things all over the world and in our own country where sometimes we have violence in the streets or weather-related disasters that wreak havoc in so many communities. We do have FEMA for some weather catastrophes, but they seem to come and go as quick as the storms. The Peace Corps would be a more hands-on, more long-term solution, and their work here and in other countries would be way more resourceful. We could have other countries build up their own Peace Corps all over the world because they will either know or find out eventually that *peace is better than war.*

I know that having a substantial Peace Corps would be somewhat costly money-wise, but here in America, it would cost a lot more to build several extra aircraft carriers with all the jets aboard it. I also know that some countries want to stay rouge like it is in North Korea and elsewhere, so we must stay on the ready for those who do not want godly peace. We must strive for more of the makings of real peace and to do that we certainly need God and Jesus Christ to be our primary influence.

In my previous books, both God and Jesus Christ have given us a lot of their full-spirited, need-to-know, proven examples with real Earth events. These are not only meant to bring us to peaceful resolutions but so that everybody can be in a much better place with God and Jesus. This also includes all nonbelievers and to those who are infected with hate, nastiness, and other ill ways. My last book, which was brought to you by God and Jesus Christ titled *The Godly Truth*, gave us a specific formula as well as seven certain prayers so that anybody who wants more peace and love and to live right to the edge of perfection for them both, can have that actually happen.

You see, God and Jesus Christ don't see war as a virtue, but they sure do give us choices to be in them or not. I even understand that someone like Hitler had to be stopped or others like him and the instigators of 9/11 had to be addressed. However, a list of five and a great worldwide Peace Corps would certainly be worth implementing. After all, just like abortions, think of how many potential doctors, inventors, scientists, and like-minded people and people living their lives day-to-day have been killed by war. People who could find other great ways to have godly peace to become a better part of our stories have possibly been killed by war.

I pray for them, I pray for you, I pray for everybody. I pray for America, our politicians, all countries, and yes, I pray constantly that great peace can be obtained. I especially always make my first prayer to be for the happiness and well-being of both God and Jesus Christ exclusively.

If you will join me in this, I'll set up the next chapter brought to you by the words of God and Jesus Christ.

4

School Days, School Nights, and In-Between

I suppose if there was a chapter that I shouldn't be able to write out for you, it would be this one, and that's because I was terrible at school. I was a prime troublemaker, and yeah, I really hated school. I especially hated it after the sixth grade because I just couldn't learn anymore. I would get stuck reading the same sentence over and over again, maybe as many as over twenty times and still get nothing out that sentence. My reading most anything was useless, and my way of spelling words or putting a sentence in order, even today, I keep the Wite-Out companies open for business.

It was discovered that my problem was being dyslexic, but back in the fifties and sixties, when I went to school, I don't think anybody knew what it was back then. Yet I live with it and am not upset with anybody but maybe myself for being a non-book-smart person. However, I just love writing out the things that God and Jesus have blessed me to bring to you by their given events, findings, circumstances, teachings, and the miracles they have allowed me to photograph. I bring them your way, not only because I love them both more than anything else in the whole wide world but also because I know that everyone's lives would be a whole lot better if every person would become their best of friends. Some people will and some won't because of the choices they make, but a better life for all can be shared if in America, our schools were way more effective.

When I went to school, it was as if you "ain't going to college," then we see you as a waste of time. Going to college or not, you are a real person and can contribute to doing something. It can be a skill, a trade, or a laborer, and the list goes on, doesn't it? Why render a person useless? The world would not work if everyone had a college degree. I mean, good luck eating if a lot of people did not work at a food processing plant or out in the fields sweating to bring us fruits and vegetables.

I could go on and on, but God and Jesus want me to share the conversations I have had with them to bring us more purposeful schools. It would start by having one or more schools in every district be open until eight at night or even a bit later. After all, a lot of tax-paying people will argue about having to pay taxes for schools they no longer attend or that their own children no longer attend either. They also pay insurance on these schools when they are *not* in use, which by the hour, is for most of any school year. Why not by the godly truth, have a lot of our schools stay open for public use after three or four o'clock, instead of locking them up? The advantages for much better societies, communities, and the like would be tremendous. After all, if you think about it, lots of teaching could still take place that could be done by retired teachers who would volunteer their services to tutor or even teach adults who simply want to learn more. I've written this before a lot of times that God and Jesus Christ always keeps it simple. These schools at night could become perfect senior citizen gathering places. If we are honest, then we do know there are a lot of lonely seniors, including some that may be in your own home, who would love to have something to do. But why end it there? What about art classes or other kinds of hobbies or learning new skills or start up community college classes or some kind or language classes? Even our police could hold meet and greets. I'll be honest, I just am not smart enough to list all the things that schools open at night could provide.

After all, you are paying the taxes and insurance for a twenty-four-hours-a-day building, but it's mostly only used about eight hours a day on a five-day week. I may not be brilliant, but to me, schools limited uses do not come out like "two plus two will equal four." Sure, there would be additional costs, but those using schools at night could offset it by nominal fees, fundraising, craft and hobby sales, donations, and other certain venues. I certainly can't put it all together, but we know that a lot of volunteering people can, and I'm sure lots of people would love to contribute.

In fact, Bible studies or various other religious teachings could also take place, even if it is said to not be politically correct. Our politicians could wander around to meet the people they are supposed to represent, and just maybe, they could learn about us. People who think staring at a smartphone all night long might just find out that there is something else to do or that there are books to read to help make all things become possible.

So…with that said and brought to all of you by God and Jesus Christ, we are going to take you to another facet that our own schools can benefit us with, not only here in America but also worldwide.

5

Let's Get Physical

I don't know about you, but when I went to school, up until the sixth grade, I loved gym or going out to play in the school yard. It was so much fun running around and fooling around. Until seventh grade, we didn't realize that was what helped us to not become obese and made us more healthy. From seventh grade on, if you didn't guess it already, I really started hating gym also. Time was spent mostly looking to see who didn't have their gym uniform on or who was not wearing gym socks with their sneakers. After a half hour wasting time checking everybody's uniform, we then had about ten minutes left to do something that was usually another waste of precious time. To me, even today, I have never seen a darling school uniform who made anybody become more physically fit!

I can't speak for what goes on in these gyms today because I am not in them, but I do know what I see. Way more kids today are way more obese than when I was at school. Even back then, schools didn't teach us about our health. Today, I think it is more about the school superintendents thinking that lots of inoculations and vaccinations will somehow make all the kids become athletic superstars. Back in my day, Down Syndrome seemed to be way less than it is today. We had no kids on the mandated psychotic medications I think are forced on kids today. Yes, we had super-hyper kids like I was, but we burned up a lot of energy in gym class if they let us play or run around outside. I don't want to dwell on that because I would much rather share with you my discussions I have had with God and Jesus about physical health. I even believe you will find that their way will make a zillion percent perfect godly sense.

It would start out in kindergarten, preschool, or whatever they call it, with a lot of the kids running around, playing physically until the fifth or sixth grade. It would then switch over to gymnastic, Olympic-type equipment to use with a lot of exercising. Karate and other martial arts that get kids physically fit can be implemented. These also teach discipline. To me, there is virtually no reason to have a lot of obese children in grade school at all. Schools can and do fail us in other areas besides education. Adults using the schools at night would create ways to get things like this discussed right to the *point of wellness.* Forgive me if I don't write it all out for you. God and Jesus are more than available to clue you in, but you gotta want to reach out to them. With them both, we will also share this for you: from sixth grade on, there would be a mandatory course on physical health and well-being. It would include, but not limited to, the healthiest foods to eat, vitamins, the dangers of smoking, drug use, drinking alcohol, and other dangers to our bodies. These courses would be mandatory because they are a necessity.

Somewhere around the ninth grade, people who have messed up their lives could come to the schools to show and tell what these awful things have done to them, their families, and so on. This could be lifesaving! Let these high school students see what their lungs and the like look like from those who died from organ damage from whatever it is that they abused. Yes, this would be a huge help to get a lot of students to learn how to respect their godly bodies.

Getting as physically fit as possible by graduation day would also lift their spirits up to be exemplary for both God and Jesus Christ, if they want them in their lives. It would also help them achieve being a nine-plus-plus as they not only get to be at the edge of perfection for God and Jesus but also for benefiting all the people in the entire world. (A nine-plus-plus was presented in my book *The Godly Truth.*)

Being physically fit, mentally fit, and spiritually fit for God and Jesus Christ is a very wonderful tribute that just might make a lot of nonbelievers think becoming very great friends with my two best friends is worth considering. As I've said, nobody has anything to lose by becoming the best of friends with God and Jesus, and nobody has anything to lose by becoming as physically, mentally, and spiritually fit as possible.

I hope that this chapter makes perfect sense to all of you, and that with faith and prayer, it will come to be. Yes, there will be some resistance, most likely from people who think that they know more than God and Jesus, but if you make a full-faith effort, then you can help them both *move mountains.* With that intentionally said, I'll give you some more of a buildup in the next chapter called "Build It: They Will Come."

<h1 style="text-align:center">6</h1>

Build It: They Will Come

If you have ever heard the expression "Build it, and they will come," then with godly determination to *build it* will become possible also. It's about building brand new cities, town, and communities instead of just expanding on the same ones we have had in America since 1850 or so. This would greatly help the United States, but building these places might just be beneficial worldwide. My God-given book mission has had me going from the east coast to the west coast for a good dozen years and also going north to south occasionally. I started putting this all together at my home in South Carolina as I keep communicating with God and Jesus Christ. I get a lot of godly satisfaction when I drive all of those many miles—if the traffic is light. Yet in all those miles, there is something else I have to speak about. In most of all these miles, there are tons and tons of empty land. I mean, it's all over the place, so much in fact it all brings us to the following simple relevant question of, why do we keep on jam-packing the same cities, town, communities, and the like with millions of more people and whatever else? Why not build a dozen new cities on vacant land? In fact, I think that all the vast empty land in Texas alone could fit in another country or two.

It takes over eight hundred miles to drive through Texas, and most of it sits barren, almost looking like another planet. A lot of other states have lots of land that sits like a chair, waiting to be sat on, so why not put this land to a much better godly use?

I know that a good share of people don't want to leave their backyard for whatever their reasons are, but consider this: If new groundbreaking ceremonies would take place to start building new cities and towns, surely people are gonna come to help build it, and maybe even stay there and live there and start a new life. Maybe such a change would help them to live a better-serving godly life. This might even help out the many immigrants who get into America by fleeing their own slipshod countries. New cities could stand on their own or be open to anyone who lives in America.

It's a very godly solution to help so many desperate people, just like those who came to America like so many of our ancestors. There would have to be checkpoints and other things to discuss, but the wisdom of God and Jesus is always available. They both expect us to have brotherly love and find ways to reach out and help. Yes, there are simple ways to fix a lot of things if we reach out to God and Jesus, but we gotta want to do it with them and for them instead of making our lives to be about ourselves. We can start to build new cities instead of being stagnant.

We can also take out the salt from the oceans with better, smarter technology, and then deliver all this fresh new water through better-built pipes that could reach all the way to the stars if need be. A lot of people could sign onto these projects and the Peace Corps, which I brought up before, could pitch in. New community kinds of service organizations could help also. The use of nonviolent people who stuff our prisons can roll up their sleeves to help, making their lives count for something. It could easily change their lives from crime as they learn new skills. Would we rather have them stay in a revolving door where nobody really wins?

I could go on and on about *build it*, but I am really not smart enough to give you all the bricks and mortar. Even if I was, I believe that you will feel a whole lot better if you roll up your sleeves to not only help both God and Jesus to move mountains but to also *fill valleys with silver linings.*

With that stated, I'll take us into the next chapter about another thing we need that I believe can use some kind of repairing, adjusting, or fixing of some kind. Yes, again the best of intentions, for this will come to us by the very blood spirit of both God and Jesus Christ. They never ever want anybody to bleed, to be crushed, or to be diminished by those who think that they can harm us in any way whatsoever.

The chapter is also telling to *God's Repair Shop*, and it's about something that haunts the streets of America and also finds a way to kill thousands, physically hurting many millions. It surely makes the safety of most any place become so questionable. The subject will be about *crime* and some simple, adjusting solutions for a way to fix it by the measures that come to us that are found within the conversations I have had with God and Jesus Christ.

Before I take you into the next chapter, I'm going to ask you a very serious question, and your answers do matter. If God and Jesus Christ will never put up with crime in heaven, then why do we have to put up with it here in America? As you think of your answer, I'll put out some repairable words in the chapter that is before you.

7

Crime No More

Because crime is such a plague on any society, it has to have two specific ways to end it. The first is by severe punishments so every dangerous criminal will know they will always serve many years doing hard work at a facility, twelve hours a day, six days a week. I'm not talking about brutal labor or treatment but work that will benefit societies and the criminals themselves. The worst and most dangerous criminals would have the job of recycling trash. Yes, let the garbage truck roll in so the thugs can get to work. If they refuse, they will get another day added to their sentence, and if they do a good day's work, maybe a day will come off. Before they are released, they will be taught a skill or trade or something to help them benefit society. (Or would you rather send them out, skilled at crime only?) The less-severe offenders could do such work as filling sandbags to help in flood areas, cut wood for distribution to help heat homes in certain areas, and so on.

Nonviolent offenders could perhaps clean up neighborhoods, cut grass, paint homes for seniors, and dozens of other tasks. The worst of the worst: killers, child molesters, rapists, those who do vicious armed robberies and other heinous crimes, could by their own choice, choose lethal injection or stay in a very small cell for the rest of their lives.

Any crime involving a gun or dangerous weapon would have a penalty of ten years just for the use of a weapon and then a certain amount of time for the crime, all without any early release. Anyone found to be a member of a violent gang would do at least five years for just belonging to a dangerous gang of that type, even if no crime was committed. I mean, can you think of a much better way to make sure violent gang membership is permanently removed from the United States and even other countries?

Convicted porch thieves, burglars, credit card thieves, identify thieves, voter fraud, and so on would have a minimum of at least five years without any early release and could spend their time recycling trash also.

It really comes down to when will we stop the *insanity* of letting our politicians talk about crime without seemingly putting their teeth into it. The solutions I've mentioned are a good starting point to teach criminals a real punishment lesson. However, the godly truth is found within the words that we will use to offset, maybe even end crime before somebody gets started in it. This is the second part of this chapter, so please feel God and Jesus in it.

Yes, by Them both, I declare that we can end crime with real godly education starting with nobody to be able to quit school except under extreme situations. Kids who cause trouble at school would have to have a parent be with them at detention because parents would give their kid a more severe punishment at home after the detention is over for making their parent sit for an hour in the detention room.

Teaching must take place where every child can only graduate by being book smart as well as trade- or skill-smart. They must also learn how to fill out mortgage and loan applications, learn about low-risk investing, and learn about the benefits of working and other life skills.

By second or third grade, children should start learning a second language. A good language should be Spanish because America has a lot of Spanish-speaking people.

With schools being open at night as I've mentioned in "School Days," our children would go there for spelling bees or special science projects. I'm sure a lot of you are starting to get this godly picture.

After graduation, all students would get the summer off and, in September, have a choice to go into any of the following four places for a mandatory year. These would be the military, the Peace Corps, community service, or a program to help senior citizens. This may sound costly, but tremendous billions have been spent to build and run prisons. Keep in mind that it costs about fifty thousand a year or more to keep just one prisoner in jail who will most likely be a criminal again when they are released. Does this insane revolving door make any sense to you?

The pay could be low for this one year of commitment to help keep the cost down, but consider this: regular schools cost around eight thousand a year per student. After twelfth grade, what do kids really know about life out in the real world? There's nothing wrong with going to college, but most likely, a lot of our children aren't going and a good bunch who do go don't make it to home plate or get a grand slam out of it.

Sorry, folks, almost 100 percent of parents will not ever get to see their college child on TV playing college football. This leaves very little room for most any child to fulfill the dream of becoming a professional athlete of any kind. However, a lot of other dreams can be had if every student comes out of school not only smart but also extremely healthy.

Yes, your input is welcome, and all of you can think about what you would want to see added here. I'm not a very smart person, and I know that many millions of you are a lot smarter than me. You can also feel free to talk about all these pages over and over with God and Jesus Christ because I do know this: I just love talking to them both every day, and I do really appreciate all that they teach me. Yes, just start talking to them because God and Jesus Christ will always and forever stay *relevant*.

8

Money, Money, Money

Would you believe me if I told you that God and Jesus really do want wealthy people? Well, I hope so because it's true. Yes, they surely do because they want wealthy people to help other people. I'm sure a lot of them do that, but I don't know if enough of them do this. I am not here to take anybody's money away from them, but I am not sure if all the super wealthy people get into godly conversations with God and Jesus Christ by prayer or seeking out their advice on what can be done for the greater good or how to invest in people. I'm sure a share of them do, and I'm sure it is the same for other people who donate, but the discrepancies about money have, in a way, plagued society in a lot of ways, haven't they? From stark outright greed, to work strikes, to die for, to swindle, to steal, and oh yeah, lots of other things also. I'm even sure money has been the cause of some wars.

We now have plastic chip cards, bitcoins, ATM machines, and ways to pay for something by the touch of a phone. None of this is an interest of mine because of what I've brought up previously. I'm just a VCR-using, cash kind of person with a flip phone, and when I was a kid, we were taught the value of money by using it somewhat wisely and no credit cards or even gift cards were around with "hook, line, and sinker" bonus points. Yet the comments of who had big money like the Rockefellers or the big corporations would jingle all over.

I'm not a smart investor guy either, but if there was one thing I could change about corporations, who go by the rule that their first obligation is to its shareholders, then it would be this: they would make their most important first obligation to God and Jesus Christ and then to America if they are American corporations or businesses. If it were that way, then China would be real far from being a super power.

I also know that God and Jesus Christ can easily increase all our blessings tenfold, especially if a person will actually live for the best interest of the both of them. Yes, real blessings from God and Jesus can really multiply and be so bountiful, especially if you serve them.

I've asked a good bunch of people this one question over the years, so now I'll ask it of you. Would you rather be very rich money-wise, or would you rather have a *rich life*? At least nine times out of ten, the question gets answered the very same way, which is, both, but only one way was asked for as somewhere in their mind they only see money as the cure all. Money can really help, but I would argue that there are lots of people who have big money that live miserable lives and have lots of problems. I can also tell you this, and it may be the most important thing that you will ever read. The *greatest wealth* that you will ever have in your life will be in the relationship that you can have with God and Jesus Christ, period! The greatest feeling that you will ever, ever have are those when you get to do something specific for them both by serving other people with the graceful act of kindness. Compassion will also especially help people who are struggling. Yes, it takes a lot more than money to change the world into a heavenly place, that's for sure, and the best way to get it to come full circle is to surround ourselves with God and Jesus Christ. To serve or do something for God and Jesus Christ either physically or spiritually, you can let their very grace for us to then overflow to many other people, other godly churches, and organizations. All of you can make the choice to work on this.

If your two best friends are not God and Jesus Christ, I would think that you, like some others, can do more for the good of all men, women, children, and the good of all countries all over the world. To me, at least, this is a better thing to do than to stare at a phone many hours of the day or to look over stock portfolios, *neither of which are required to get anybody a place in heaven.*

I'm sure that these first eight chapters have spiritually lifted your insights to see that God and Jesus are clearly on our side, and that we all have a choice to have many great victories with them. As all of you relish in that thought, I will go to the next part of this God-given book. It will be about more of the events that God and Jesus have created and really happened shortly after they made the crown of Jesus Christ in the sky during March of 2013. The picture of that very crown can be seen right on the cover of their first book titled *A Crown for Jesus*, so check it out. These several events really took place, and as I've told you not too long ago, we would bring them to you. Both God and Jesus never ever keep anything from you, but they also never overload anybody by giving them too much at once. They only go by their own exclusive timing, and this truly is a great time to receive more information that only they both can bring your way from the well-founded spirited events that they have made possible. So if you are ready for this next event story from them, it will be a real eye-opener, then I'll get right into it in the next chapter.

9

Half Person, Half Angel

To be honest with you, I can't be date-specific about this event because as some of you already know, I don't stockpile any specific notes, write in a journal, or have a secretary. No, I just go with the flow that has me hanging out with God and Jesus, and I try hard not to annoy them. I can't even tell you why they chose me for any of this because I lack every credential that you would think that would be needed to do anything for them. The great news about this is it's more than living proof that *anyone* of you, in fact, can actually do things physically or spiritually for them, especially if your faith and your desire is to love them way more than anything else.

Let me also assure you that my journey with God and Jesus Christ, since I made a choice to believe in them both, has not always been a piece of cake or a bowl of cherries. I'm sure that the trials of my life have challenged God and Jesus to even say, "It's time to give up on this guy." But here is the godly truth. God and Jesus Christ never ever give up on anybody at all. They both have made the many events in my life to be way beyond the fascination or curiosity that anyone could ask for. They have made some events to be very life-challenging, dangerous, and very excruciating. They are, however, learning and teachable experiences.

This "half person, half angel" event will *not* put a happier day in your life, but you will surely gain something from it. I can't give you a specific time or date, but it took place somewhere in 2016. It took place in northern Florida in a backyard where I occasionally hang out. It has some big, peaceful oak trees and is usually relatively quiet.

I do my best to focus on God and Jesus Christ because I really love hanging out with them way more than anything else.

It was a nice, sunny day with a few scattered clouds in the sky. I looked at a bigger one, and it was kind of "plain Jane" but was also in the shape of a box. God and Jesus told me to pay attention to it, so I did. Suddenly, a huge arm with a hand came out of one side of it and a huge angel's wing came out of the other side. I was kind of relating to it, but I asked myself, *What is this about?* God and Jesus said to look at the top of it, and suddenly a neck and huge head appeared. I instantly knew that right then, I was looking at a cloud that transitioned into a half person and half angel, but the face had no features at all. In about another minute, a very big smile appeared on the angel side of the face and the half person had a huge frown on it. They were attached at the midway point, and you can be assured I was really paying strict attention to it all.

I mean, I knew that God and Jesus had a reason to show me this, but they were not telling me why at this time. I kept staring, and the smile on the angel half got bigger, and I could tell that it was extremely happy. However, the person side's frown turned into a state of incredible pain. Horror was written all over that half, and it just kept getting worse and worse. I looked at its arm with its hand, and it was twisting and turning because the human half was experiencing the pain as if it was on fire. Yes, the human half was in such massive pain to the point of where it was as if millions of vicious bees and scorpions were stinging it over and over again a billion times a second right to the point of where I could feel it, not only affecting me emotionally but also in a certain godly, spirited way. I was feeling so devastated, but then God and Jesus said to look at the angel half again, so I did.

The relief was so extraordinary that I could never be able to find any appropriate words in the world's biggest dictionary to be able to describe it for you. Yes, the angel part of the face had a smile from the all-out happiness of heaven. As I took a quick look at the person half, I could see, as plain as day, all its horror and all its tremendous pain was coming from the very depths of hell. I just concentrated on the angel half because I fully understood that this is where God and

Jesus Christ intend for us to be. They were also reinforcing in myself and my spirit for them that no matter what our feelings are, they give everyone the very same thing which is *choice*.

They were also telling me that this "half person, half angel" event was letting me know that mathematically, if each person averages about ten sins a day and then you multiply it by the seven billion people on this Earth, then God and Jesus witness over seventy billion sins a day. Just think of how very excruciating that is for them and how it emotionally affects them. The choices for our behavior does truly affect them just like they can affect everybody in the world.

I've written before that God and Jesus Christ see everything that we do. There is *nothing* that we can hide from them, but we can make choices to sin less today than we did yesterday. In fact, in my third book titled *God's Cabin*, there is a specific chapter called "Sin Less than Before." This will give us a great platform to explicitly sin a lot less. My fourth book, *The Godly Truth*, has a very specific formula to help anybody to live right to the very awesome edge of perfection for God and mighty Jesus Christ. I'm not trying to promote these books, but these really are *their* books, their events, stories, photographs, findings, and more.

At a seventh-grade level of education, I'm not even sure I'll ever qualify as a well-written author, but I really do my best to write out the words God and Jesus give me so we can always give them all of their well-deserved respect and full-time glory. I do my best so that all of you can truly become a huge part of the great big God and Jesus Christ story. I know that anybody but a fool would much rather be in an angel cloud than a cloud that only provides for the dark misery of hell.

It's not hard to ever have a tremendous relationship with God and Jesus Christ. They both keep everything simple. They both love all of us way more than anybody ever can or ever will, and they want all of us to be with them, not only on this Earth but also forever in heaven.

This brings up the call of where you are spending your time and who you are spending your time with. Yes, it can be rough out there in the world, even painful, but anybody is allowed to find a *comfort zone* in God and Jesus Christ physically or spiritually; better yet, even both, but you gotta really want to do that. Staring at a phone all day may give you some satisfaction, but it will never be better than getting to know God and Jesus Christ a whole lot better.

Yes, God and Jesus Christ clearly give us choices, so if you would like to make an effective choice for them, please help take away some of their pain from the seventy billion or more sins that they will see today and read the next event chapter. It will help boost up your confidence and help assure us that both God and Jesus Christ have the essentials to give us the very foundation to increase or start a relationship with them.

10

A Great Big Smile

Sorry, but once again, I can't be specific about the date, but if my memory is correct, I'm pretty sure this happened in 2017 or 2018. I was spending some time at a senior mobile home park near Daytona Beach, Florida, where God and Jesus had already made two very great things for me to witness. One was the showcasing of the crown of Jesus Christ and the other was a very spectacular rainbow. This new happening in its own way was quite different because it took place at night. The sun was down for a couple of hours, and at around 8:00 p.m., I decided to get on my bike and go to the clubhouse to see a friend of mine who was over ninety years old and a World War II veteran.

As I took my bike out the door, God, for his *reasons*, told me to put the bike inside and to walk. I kind of hesitated and started to get on my bike because I really wanted to ride because the weather was so perfect to ride my bike. But then, Jesus stepped in and He, with God, got very serious about them wanting me to put the bike back and to walk to the clubhouse. I knew better than to argue with them or to get mad at them for any reason whatsoever. So I did what they asked of me, and I'm sure glad that I did. By walking, I was able to look up at the sky instead of only looking forward, which is the position all bike riders have their eyes in most of the time.

You see, as I looked up, God and Jesus put on another very tremendous showcasing event, which is so awesome to describe. All the clouds were deep-scarlet, bloodred, signifying the color of the blood that Jesus shed for all of us. Only one huge cloud was brilliant white and had a full spirited shine to showcase the light of God that he so badly wants us to have in full earnest. It is a light of God's protective armor to shield us away from those who want to take us away from them. It can also help guide us to the pathway to heaven. From this event and some of their other ways of teaching, God and Jesus want all of us to know the following: The very blood of Jesus Christ is always available to every single human being that is born. It is also inside of every aborted embryo. This very blood of Jesus is also found in those who are adopted, so please whoever you are, never ever over look that.

To deliver a life is a beautiful victory, and only a woman can be blessed to do that in the light of God, period. For any woman who can't physically have a baby, then the act of adoption is a great victory also. In fact, as they were revealing this to me, I looked at the moon, and what I saw was so fantastic. The moon had grown well over four times bigger than any full moon I had ever seen in almost my seventy years of life. It also had a great big smile on it, not just because I put my bike away, but to let us all know of how much God and Jesus cares about us. This moon was smiling way wider than the Grand Canyon ever could, and I sure was enjoying all the miles the smile had.

Right now, you or anybody else can become a huge part of that super smile if you will simply increase your friendship with God and Jesus Christ or let yourself become a first-time friend with them. This, too, is so godly victorious.

They both are never about steadfast consistent doom and gloom that somehow gets imposed on us—an imposition that seems media-driven as they rarely report on God or Jesus Christ. Everybody can put the blood of Jesus Christ to use and have the light of God to shine on them to become a better person so that the edge of perfec-tion becomes prevailing and the right-spirited ways of our lives will increase. It's not that hard to do if you are *wanting* this, not only for yourself and others but also for God and Jesus Christ. They both are *exceptional*. They never make themselves hard to find. You simply have to want them both more than anything else in your life and then really get to know them.

Now that you know that, I'll go into the next chapter, and it will show you that I am never ever perfect. Yes, I do know some things about God and Jesus Christ, but I do muck up a lot. I specialize in keeping myself limited, and that's why there are no photographs for the previous God-given stories. This next event story will end up without a picture also, but I do think you will see all its colors that God and Jesus want us to enjoy.

11

A Second Time Event

Once again, I can't be date-specific, but I can get pretty close because I headed to Arizona to be with God and Jesus sometime in May 2018. There was one thing puzzling me about something that I forgot to get before I left my primary home in South Carolina, but I just could not figure out what it was. I even had it on my list of things to bring with me, and soon, all of you shall know what it was. I don't think any of you will ever forget this event because God and Jesus Christ made something so explicitly beautiful. It was so beautiful that when I am done with this chapter, if you close your eyes and open your imagination, I'm certain you will see it. I'm certain that you will see exactly how God and Jesus made it, and you will also know that it's purpose is to get people out of the dark and get to the edge of perfection for my two best friends.

I had just gotten off I-10 in New Mexico after the sun came up. When I got to Silver City, New Mexico, I stopped for gas and to fill up my big coffee mug. I stretched my legs and body extensively because I had been driving about twenty hours with just a couple of quick naps in the back seat of my car. I was nowhere near tired. The sun was way up high, and there was not one cloud in the sky. I started driving again, heading north, and about an hour later, this event took place. It was still early in the day, and I had only seen a car or two because I was on this very beautiful scenic back road. As desolate as this road was, it also was a great shortcut to where *God's Cabin* proudly sits and where God and Jesus enjoy hanging out.

The sun was still on a full light display, and there were still no clouds anywhere. The ground, for as far as I could see, was as dry as if it had not been rained on recently. I was conversing quite intensely with God and Jesus because it comes naturally to me on the open road, especially when there are almost no cars around or any other distractions. I was really enjoying my time with God and Jesus, and then they said to look toward a rather small mountain on the left side of the road, which I did and man, oh man, they started making something astronomically incredible.

Out of the ground about midway up the mountain, a rainbow was in the process of being born. I pulled over on the side of this back country road to watch a *rainbow in the making*. It was, for sure, one of the most breathtaking, godly beautiful things they ever gave me to witness and to describe to you. Minute by minute, it grew from the ground and got larger and larger until it fully arched for a good twenty miles across. It touched down right into a field of almost waist-high grass that suddenly looked like super golden strands of hair. The intense array of colors then glowed with the vividness of a purity that lit up the virgin grass, making it look like golden fire. I was just flabbergasted, almost gasping for air, and then God and Jesus told me to look at the mighty arch. I did, and there is virtually no way to ever come up with the millions of greatest words for me to describe it to you.

I can tell you this: each color had its own distinctive joy. Every color was way beyond happy and were extremely proud of themselves. I could see that they were so ecstatic to be sharing their faithfulness to touch each other, and yes, they were radiating back and forth, letting us know that getting along with each other is not meant to ever be complicated. Yes, God and Jesus were not only reaching me but also teaching me during this exuberating moment, that all of us can touch each other in the purest colors of great brotherly love.

I could go on and on about this rainbow for another half hour because that's the godly truth of how long it lasted. I also would have taken a full twenty-seven pictures of it because that's how many frames a disposable camera has. However, I didn't do that because I told you that I forgot to get something when I left for this trip, and yeah, it still bothers me. *Forgetting that camera* really hurt, and it really bothered me for many days because I have never learned to use the camera on my flip phone, even to this day as I'm writing this. I did try to use it for that rainbow. I took a picture of a blur, but please don't ever blur out God and Jesus from your life. They both are *superior*. They are all the colors of the rainbow and everything more. They both make all these radiant colors for all of us, so why not accept them? Why not do something with them? Why not use them for their purpose by making a superior choice to get along with everybody?

You see, in book 1, *A Crown for Jesus*, they both made an ultra-certain rainbow to teach that all of us can live in the colors of Their life to keep us out of the very dark that hurts and harms us. In God's truth, it doesn't have to be that way if the right choices are made, but you gotta wanna make them. Learning and living for them both is not ever complicated, and they sure can teach us by the peaceful colors of their rainbows.

12

A Breath of Fresh Air

Before I bring you into the scope of this chapter, I am sure a lot of you are still in at least one color of the rainbow in chapter 11, so I'll also share this about it. This was the only time to date that God and Jesus Christ made a specific similar event for me to witness twice. Once again, they have more than made it clear about the importance of us all getting along and to stay out of the dark imposed on us by other people or governments who are *not* living in the godly truth. You also have to understand that there was *not* a single cloud in the sky, no moisture of any kind to make this rainbow, and that its very purpose happened for a teachable moment. Learning all we can from God and Jesus directly is more than possible, and it starts out by your willingness to communicate with them. I think that any clear-minded person is gonna see this new chapter and will certainly have some things to know or think about no matter what position that a person sides with.

The controversial subject will be about the battling sides of global warming or climate change. We have those who scream that it does exist and those who say "No way," and others who push it aside. Well, I do know exactly what it is by the very conversations I've had with God and Jesus. It is *pollution change*, and I will prove it to you by the way of God's question: Do you really think that we can pollute our air, water, and other resources that God has blessed us with for over a hundred years without any earthly or living kind of damages? I am not a scientist or weatherman to give you any of the data for what unabated pollution is doing for this or that, but I can tell you what I do know or have experienced. For starters, when I was growing up in Queens and Long Island, New York, we really had four greats seasons of weather, and the streams and beaches were spotless. I was around twelve years old when they shut down Alhambra and Florence Beach because the water got so polluted. This happened when I got back from Vietnam. Instead of four fabulous seasons of weather, it started raining almost constantly, and the sky was mostly cloudy gray most of the time. I mean, it really sucked, that's for sure.

When I was ten years old, I remember my father saying not so good things about all the car exhaust fumes and the eight-inch chimney flues from so many houses that burned almost raw oil to heat their homes with no filters and no scuffing screens—just black smoke going up into the air. I even remember the black bits of grime that would stick to my face on the New York city streets and this was fifty or sixty years ago! Yet we still have deniers who flick this aside by commenting "so what" or if a volcano goes off, just saying "look at all the soot." (As if that's a good reason to pollute and not care about it.)

I'm not a scientist or a smart person, but I at least know enough to admit that something is wrong or has gone out of whack. I talk to God and Jesus a real, real lot, and I know that they are not happy about it either. They always teach us about being clean and pure. I also know that through them, by the use of their grace, their collective wisdom and spirited knowledge, vast encouraging improvements can be made. Letting them be our best source of inspiration can lead to more certain rainbows for living, not only for each other but with each other.

Everything can be done if we put *God's Repair Shop* to use, but we just gotta wanna do it instead of ripping each other apart. Even the "misery first" media people can tone it down, and they can certainly bring up God and Jesus Christ on an everyday basis. Tearing each other apart is not conducive to the teaching of God and Jesus Christ because they only specialize in the very positive thinking and *building people up*.

Not everything is a false narrative, and each side should be heard at bare minimum. There is a right way to do that, and it can*not* be with devoted hatred. Hatred is never going into God's heaven, so why not drop it? In fact, hatred in and of itself is such a perverted pollution, just like pollution on Earth is. There are minds way brighter than mine to curtail or end all pollution so let's pray for them to accomplish this. We also need to know that both God and Jesus monitor how we treat the gift of Earth to us on an everyday basis. Yes, they see everything. This gives them a verification of how much every person will have for respecting heaven that God has created for us.

With that written out, I'm going to go into another chapter that will almost marry up to the great pollution debate that so many of the world's politicians seem to choke on.

13

Politically Speaking

I know that some people don't want to talk about this, and there are some who can't help themselves, so politics for them is like a verbal diet. I am not an expert about politics either, but like so many people in the USA, we know that politicians in Washington seem to be way off the rail. I'm to the point where I only vote for *Jesus Christ*, and yeah, I hope you might want to know why. However, before I get into all that, I've been told that I'm wasting my vote, I'm crazy, and a list of other foolish things.

But let me ask you a few simple questions. In our current political battlegrounds, do you think that God is offended by me because I only vote for his godly son Jesus? Do you think he is mad at me or thinks I am out of my mind? Do you think that God and Jesus hate the signs I've put on my lawn that say *"Only vote for Jesus Christ"* and *"Put all your faith in God, not politics"*?

I can tell you this: A lot of people really do love both of these signs. Some take pictures of them so that people all over the world can see them. People honk their horns in very real spiritual happiness. People shout from their car windows, *"Amen!"* Some stop to talk to me, and we have great conversations about the only real king that will forever be Jesus Christ, and yes, I give all of them a photo of the picture that God with Jesus made for all of us: the crown of Jesus Christ that they made in the sky in March of 2013. It proudly sits on the cover of my first book titled *A Crown for Jesus*. I also get to hand out some of the other great pictures that God and Jesus created and blessed me to take so that you can find a way to see them. Some are on the covers of other books I have written, and if you want to spend some quality time with God and Jesus, then you can make a choice to read them.

These are *their stories*, so why not join them because in essence, all of these books were developed by both of them so that they can really become *your stories*. You might even find that your relationship will grow from them in a whole new spirited way or that a first-time friendship with God and Jesus is a lot better than putting all your faith in the many politicians of today. You see, I just can't find a path to any politician who has put America into debt of nearly thirty trillion dollars or one who has maybe become a bedfellow to China or who keeps the doors wide open for abortion to exist or those who tell you that they are against it but for the past fifty years has allowed this kind of mass killing of a new potential life and is still taken from us by the "same old, same old." These kinds of talkers have had over twenty years of their own political president, but fetuses are still killed every day.

I'll say it again by asking this question. How would you feel if Jesus Christ was ripped out of the womb of Mary before he was approaching his day of birth? In fact, I'm sure if that was going to be the end of his life, any rational person would have loved to see him saved by *instant adoption*. Yes, a very serious challenge that hopefully will be made into law by the people I cannot vote for, but if they do, then just maybe that can change my mind a little bit. There are other issues that come up empty, like never hearing a politician say that their first obligation is to God and Jesus Christ and then to all of us.

I'm not going to go into a whole lot more specifics, and I will never tell you who you have to vote for, but please consider this: Since I started voting for Jesus Christ fifty years ago, I feel so much more enlightened. I'm meeting more and more people every year who only vote for Jesus, and they have a proud, spirited glow in their eyes. They have the full confidence of going to heaven even though, like me, they are not ever perfect people. Like me, however, they really love showing their full, spirited dedication to Jesus by voting for him. Our real devotion, our full faith show us a way to give God and Jesus Christ all *the glory*, all the time. In fact, voting for Jesus Christ is really catching on. I have seen quite a few signs on other lawns that say "*Vote for Jesus.*" I've even seen billboards saying the same thing, and it feels so spectacular and so very good that I can make you this spirited godly promise. If you will vote for Jesus Christ in an upcoming or future election and then look in the mirror, you're going to see yourself in a whole new way, and you're going to appreciate both God and Jesus more than you ever have before. All you have to do is try it, and I know that you will find out that you will make God and Jesus happier than the day before. So why not try voting for just only Jesus Christ once in your life?

Voting for God and Jesus really has a pure, Christian ring of truth to it, doesn't it? I'll share this with you also, no politician any-where in the world or any world leader of any kind has the power to place you or anybody into the greatest place in God's heaven. Only Jesus Christ can do that for any of us, and this could be an extra special reason to vote for Him. It comes from the choices we make, and all of us know because we are not ever perfect, that we do need to make better choices. This is not to say that all politicians are bad or evil people, and they, like everybody else, have to be prayed for.

I'm sure that being a person in Congress or the Senate or even the president of the United States is not as easy as one, two, three, especially with the media people who, on any given day, may find a way to spew word-hating adjectives or any other words to make us feel forever hopelessly divided. To me, it's a pathetically driven shell game for bigger ratings, higher paychecks, egos, and some other pro-nouns of hateful dividing that God and Jesus might just add into the pile of over seventy billion sins a day. Certainly, God and Jesus Christ not only hear everything we say but also know all the intentions of each and every syllable. They both always know of the good, the bad, and the ugly, and neither will ever be in heaven at all, just like hate will never be there either.

Your salvation will be in heaven given by Jesus Christ and not one media person can ever put you there either. I'm not saying that it is the media's agenda to put us in hell, but even here, we have a choice. That choice is that any person can stay glued to the TV screen for hours upon hours, watching the nasty negativity or any person can instead give that precious time to God and Jesus Christ to people in need or a mission like not having schools closed after 3:00 or 4:00 p.m. as specified in chapter 4.

I'm sure that a handful of politicians would join us on that venture, and then we can all team up on the next one. I even believe that God and Jesus would really like that a lot, and so would the politicians who commit themselves to a real God and Jesus project like this as they look forward to becoming united. Doing things for the best interest of God and Jesus could really catch on, and I think a few media people might just speak highly of this new way of talking, finally bringing up more and more good news stories instead of all the worst news after the bad news. A new better valued way to influx Christianity so that maybe a way of political speaking could lift up all our spirits and to give God and Jesus a *well-deserved break*. As all of you think about that, also think of something, anything that you can put together for *God's Repair Shop* because I have no way to fix every broken-down car on the road or one that has sat for years in a backyard.

I also have to write out a few more chapters for you because if you have gotten this far, then I'm sure that you're wanting to read them. I promise that these upcoming chapters will not be the stern or boring lectures that I had to put up with in high school that had me staring at the clock for the exact second that I could finally get out of there. I believe that you will see the real truth in the upcoming chapters because some will give you an extraordinary taste for heaven and a need to know and some things to think about. All my stories have come to you by the direct way of God and Jesus Christ so I don't think you will find any one of them to be off center or to leave you disillusioned. In fact, you even get a choice to choose any of them or all of them to become a part of your very own special God and Jesus Christ story.

I'll have this new chapter to be one that will put a lot more beautiful, godly colors in your life. It is a beautiful presentation that sparkles just like the rainbow that all of you read about to be for our benefit, so get ready for this event, and please pay attention because something kind of happens twice.

14

Wings of Beauty

To tell you the truth, this is mostly not my story. It came to me from a woman I met due to the very nature of God and for his absolutely full-spirited reasons. I met this pleasant woman who was in her forties at a comfortable place in Ormond Beach, Florida. It took place in the early spring in 2018. We were conversing gingerly because we started talking about when somebody dies. I told her about the crown photo and got her one from my car. She looked at it with full belief because she was a true believer in God and Jesus Christ. I told her the story about that picture, and then she told me a story about herself that was so fascinating.

Her favorite thing in her life from God are butterflies. One day, she was in a huge country field talking with God and Jesus. The grass she sat on was so soft and very comfortable, she laid down and prayed until she went to sleep. Some time had passed by, and while she was still sleeping, she started to hear the softest sound of wings fluttering all around her. It got louder and louder until it fully woke her up. As she rose from the ground, her eyes were completely dazzled because God had filled the sky all around her with billions of incredibly beautiful butterflies. They were as far as her eyes could see through the narrow spaces between them. There were big ones and small ones and had many brilliant, extravagant colors; certain colors that had clearly just come from heaven because she had never seen them before. She then stretched out her arms to fully praise God and Jesus and then thousands of butterflies landed softly on them. They soon became like a full body cast as they swarmed in to cover her entire body. This went on for about ten minutes, and just like many others who have experienced the extraordinarily blessed events with God and Jesus, she will never ever forget it. Blessings are really there to be had, but you gotta really want them to be in your life. As I've written from them both to all of you, God and Jesus Christ know what our hearts want and need way more than we even do. They can make anything possible if you believe.

In fact, I fully believed her story so much that both God and Jesus took this butterfly story a *little bit further*. I never forgot her story, and sometimes I talk to God and Jesus about it. I bring it up to them at God's Cabin also. It's placement in the Arizona desert where it sits usually has the grace of a few butterflies to visit the flowers that grow in every direction. On this particular day, I was conversing with my two greatest heavenly friends where the area was mostly barren ground. It only had a few weather-beaten bushes that just had a few leaves on them. All the bushes were the exact same kind, and they all looked like they were past their prime.

I was thinking about that woman, and suddenly a butterfly landed on one of the drab bushes. It was about ten feet away from me. Then another one landed, and soon, many other butterflies also landed on it. I was really enjoying this because I could feel God and Jesus's spirit in this moment. Suddenly, more and more butterflies kept coming, landing on this bush until there was no room to land on it anymore. I knew what was happening, but I looked at the other same type bushes that were here and there, not one had a butterfly. Even more butterflies came, and when one left the bush, another took its place. This went on for a few hours until I got up to go to the cross and beautiful rock formation that I had placed by God's cabin. I fully thanked them and gave them both all the greatest glory for another miraculous event that they gave explicitly for all of us.

I must ask you, can any of you think of anything more *peaceful* than a gentle butterfly or even billions of them? If they surround you or fully cover you, they will always go easy on you just like God and Jesus want to be easy on all of us. However, how easy do we collectively or individually want to cover Them both with sin free behavior? It is upon us to do or not to do all the many nasty things on this Earth that greatly offend God and Jesus Christ every day. They both clearly see the darkest over seventy billion sins we have on a daily basis. I could go on with this, but I would rather bring the real peace of a butterfly to God and Jesus Christ. It just takes consistent peaceful, beautiful choices. So why not offer that to them? Why not live the godly truth that can bring anybody to the edge of perfection for both of them and for each other?

God and Jesus always make hundreds, if not thousands, of spirit-telling events every day throughout the world. They heal people, they save lives, and they even have a heaven waiting for us. In the last chapter, I pointed out that it is time for us to *give both God and Jesus a break* so let's get started in doing that.

We need to have them both be our very first priority, to be the first that we pray for instead of making it about ourselves or of me, me, me. If you want a better life, a better country, or a better world, it starts with God and Jesus Christ, period. Many have tried to do it without them and never pray for their happiness or their well-being. America is supposed to be a strong Christian nation, but the average person in it knows that it is not as pretty as a butterfly anymore. It even lacks those words called *peace for all.* That does not mean that it all has gotten away from us, but putting more colors in our lives and into the lives of God and Jesus can surely do us no harm. Transformation takes time. It takes patience, and it takes perverseness. It may take even a few more things, but I am nowhere near smart enough to figure that all out.

However, I at least know this, that anyone of us or even all of us can fix our lives for the better somewhere in *God's Repair Shop.* As you contemplate that, I'll set up the next chapter because it is special in its own way and will give us more teachable moments.

15

The Popcorn Lady

This is going to be different because I think it will put God's heaven on your mind. It took place in Arizona at a small senior campground where most of these campers and motor homes are permanently set up. Most of them have additions, decks or other stuff added to them so they will have the effect of being like a cabin. I was spending the summer here about three years ago, and I was in the laundry room when an older woman came in. I could see that she had a lot of pride, but in God's truth, she was dressed kind of ragtag, but I didn't give that a lot of thought; perhaps because my clothes will tell you that my wardrobe comes from a variety of thrift stores. In fact, God and Jesus have blessed me to find a thrift store where anything off the rack is only a dollar. It is run by a minister who preaches and teaches God's Word, and from time to time, we have really great and important godly conversations.

In the laundry room, this elderly woman and I looked at each other, and she started straightening out the magazines. Then she said, "I won't be long, and I will not get in your way." I said, "If you need me to move, just tell me because I'm not doing anything important." Then she said, "I have to change out some of these magazines so I'll be back with some more."

Before she left (for God's reasons), this lady and I just started talking about God and Jesus Christ. The conversation was terrific so I brought up the crown of Jesus photo. She said she would love to see it, but I told her I could do better than that and I would go and get her one she could have. I told her it would take me about twenty-five minutes before I could get back with it, but you can be sure I'll be here because I know that you will really love it. She said this was fine because she had to go back to her camper to get the change of magazines. Then she smiled so wide and said, "I just really love doing this." For some reason, the stupid in me asked, "Do they pay you much for doing that?" She then smiled wider, and with the glow of Jesus written all over her, she said, "No, I volunteer and I'm more than happy to do this here and at a few other places too."

That made me smile as I said, "Well, I'll be back in about twenty-five minutes. She said that would be perfect because it would give her time to eat her dinner. I then said, "If you're going to eat dinner, then don't hurry because I can come back even later." She smiled effortlessly but with a certain stellar pride and said, "No, twenty-five minutes is fine because I am just having *popcorn*."

I said, "Popcorn!" And without any harmful intentions, I said "Popcorn" again. I quickly said, "What kind of dinner is that?"

She proudly said, "It's okay, I eat it for dinner almost every night."

I was stunned because to me, for a senior to east mostly popcorn for dinner almost every night is not what the great American dream is about. I offered to take her out to dinner or to get her some kind of takeout or get her some groceries, but with her greater godly pride, she stood tall and just kept saying, "No, that's okay, I will be fine. I am used to it." She then said, "All I really want is for you to get me the picture that you said is *the crown of Jesus Christ*." I left and got it, and when I saw her about twenty-five minutes later, I handed it to her. So let me speak clearly!

I just have to tell you that you never saw a happier, prouder person in all of your life. Her happy tears sparkled way better than all the stars at night. I mean, you just had to be there to feel God and Jesus Christ in the room. In fact, it's not hard to feel them both right now because they both feel it in all of us. I think that some of you can smell the very essence of that popcorn and even get a taste for what she is gonna say soon.

We continued talking about God and Jesus Christ, about how awesome they both are and how they can really make all things to be possible. We continued to talk about God's great heaven and how we might get to see each other there. I just had to ask her, "Well, when I get to heaven, if you are already there, how will I find you?"

She just smiled and said, "It will be easy to find me because I'll always be passing out magazines." Let me ask, does this surprise you? They both have already let some people know what they will be doing in heaven. Without bragging, I have proven so many times that they know what your heart really wants, but for them to deliver, *your heart really has to want them.*

Anybody can be the poorest person in the world or be homeless living under a bridge, but they can also be super rich in a greater relationship with God and Jesus Christ. Even big-time-money people can have a very wealthy relationship with God and Jesus just like anybody can. We can also have a satisfactory blessing if we will help those who would give an eye-tooth for a bag of popcorn.

There are charities in need, veterans in need, families in need, and the list can pop right out of the bag. Yes, the American dream is available, but if we still allow thousands of our children to quit school and leave without a real skill, trade, or a realistic education, there will be a lot more bags of popcorn eaten for dinner. We have to do more than a few things mentioned in chapter 4, but are we, in the name of God and Jesus, gonna pop and hop to it? I know I've brought up education several times, but when you read this next chapter, all of you will clearly get the picture of why.

16

The Story of Three

Isn't it amazing how God and Jesus will let us experience things in the past and keep them in our memory pocket? Any of these things can have or lead to different outcomes, and some of them can put us into a better-spirited life for God and Jesus. I'll start with this first true story, and it might just drop your jaw.

I had moved to South Carolina in 1990. One of the nearby neighbors was a young woman, about twenty-five years old. She told me that she just recently gotten her first job as a schoolteacher. Her eyes lit up as she said God had blessed her for her heart's desire.

Being that I was from the north, I had never heard of any great things about the Southern education system, so I asked her, "What are the schools like in this area?"

She looked flustered like she didn't want to tell me but then said when she went to her interview for her first teaching job, the principal asked her this question. "What are your goals for how you want to teach your students?" Her reply was "to give them the best education that I can." The principal said, "No, no, no," and she thought something was wrong. So the principal asked her again what her goals were, and her reply was the same as before: "To give the students the very best that I can." She then added to help all of them become as smart as possible. The principal again said, "No, no, no." She looked at him, sort of confused, and then asked him, "Why do you keep saying 'No, no, no'? Isn't that what you expect me to do? Don't you want me to give my students a great education and for them to become smart?"

His answer will shock the heck out of you, so take a deep breath of air because you will need it. He said to her at a zillion percent these very words: "No, we do not want smart students because when they leave school and go to work, then they will want more *money*." She was so taken aback by his answer; it literally crushed her. Her heart was really shattered and most likely still is because this is not how she wanted to teach. She then told me she would never break her vow to God and Jesus Christ in any other way but to give her students the best education possible.

Think of how cruel that principal's words of "no, no, no" were. Was this just his policy, or was it the whole educational system's policy for South Carolina? I mean the South back then, and perhaps even today if I am not mistaken, comes up really low in the national statistics for the bragging rights for producing well-educated students.

To make such a statement to any teacher and to believe in it by this principal, a school district, or if it's a policy of any state, is extremely cruel and outright dangerous. To me, it is evil and you can be sure God and Jesus *document all of it*. It is also anti-God and Jesus Christ, and I'll tell you why. Purposely keeping people dumbed down causes *oppression*, and any person of God and Jesus should absolutely know for a fact that the both of them are extremely against oppression. It can cause crime, the spread of disease, war, and the list could most likely wrap around the world.

Sadly, that's true because just think of how many illiterate poor countries that you don't want to live in. Even in Afghanistan, they refuse to get smart enough to let women become very educated. Yet here in America, our educational teaching by world statistics, if I am not mistaken, are nowhere near number 1. (Why is that?) However, I did tell you there would be three specific stories in this chapter, so I'll drop your jaw again with the second one. This comes from seeing with my own eyes.

I went to a lumber yard at the edge of the North Carolina, South Carolina border. I paid for a dozen boards that I wanted. The clerk at the desk looked at the other clerk and sort of jokingly said that I may have to help the person outside to help me load up. Then he and the other clerk just stared, laughing, but I did not know why, but I soon found out. When I handed the person (who was in his forties) the receipt for the purchase, he just stared at me and did nothing. I said to him, "That slip is for the lumber I need and already paid for." He still did nothing, and this went on for another minute and *then it hit me*; he could not read! I could see that it bothered him, but let me tell you what bothered me. It was those two clerks inside that were laughing about it. I was also really upset that the school system failed him and us and sadly did not educate him to be able to read. I talked to this man, and he said that he grew up in North Carolina. I could give you other specifics to our conversation, but I'll tell you this instead. Sometimes, at a couple of jobs that I had in South Carolina, I had the responsibility of taking money as well as checks. I would at times have to write out these checks because the adults could not do it themselves or did not know how to sign their name.

How pathetic to let people, white or black or any color, race, religion, or anything else you can think of, go through most of their life, uneducated. Some of you might say, "Well, that was ten, twenty, or thirty years ago," but the third story will bring all of you up to date and may have your heart skip a beat.

It happened in 2020 up the road on a street where I spend a few weeks in Florida during the winter. It is near the I-10 interstate corridor, close to the Florida-Georgia line and about thirty-five miles from Alabama. It's also an area of low-paying jobs, and its scenery, although quite beautiful, has lots of older, single-wide mobile homes.

Just up the street from me is a tall teenage guy who lives in a trailer with his mom. He has a basketball hoop set up and he practices a lot. I love watching him because he hit the basket quite often. On a school day and during school hours, he came walking by. I felt something was wrong because I'd see him get on the school bus sometimes. I called out to him and said, "Hey, John, no school today?"

He said, "No."

I replied, "Really? Why is that because I saw the school bus go by earlier?"

Now before I tell you the next part of our conversation, you need to get ready for it because it is almost unbelievable.

John said, "Well, actually, they kicked me out of school because I got left back."

I said, "That's the stupidest thing I ever heard. Anybody can get left back, and getting left back should not matter."

Then John put his head down and said in a dispirited way, "Well, they said it was because I was *nineteen* and still in the *ninth* grade."

I could only say "Really!" I was flabbergasted and then it hit me. The blame for this was not his alone.

Where were the parents, the teachers, the school system because something really has to have a lot of wrongs to have a nineteen-year-old who is still in the ninth grade. I thought of what his future would look like. Would it be drugs, drinking, crime, and a fill of the lowest-paying jobs? How could something like this benefit our country?

We know that tons of school districts spend exuberant amounts of money on sports teams and fancy schools, but how many of our schools have after-hour school tutors? Yeah, it may be glamorizing to believe that our own children will become the next Lebron James or the next great female athlete. For the few that our educational dollars are spent on to make this happen, what about the millions that will never be in any kind of professional sport or even a high-dollar sportscaster?

I'm sure that you will agree that crime, drinking, drug use, or any other thing that a poor education leads to is dangerous, yet the three stories I shared with you are real and, in fact, tragic. When you multiply those stores by the hundreds of thousands, it becomes obvious to the plague of so many people being homeless, which is an ever-present American story that may very well continue on unless all of us make much better *choices*. Yes, the word choices always stays relevant just like the question, *What if Jesus Christ had been killed by abortion?*

As we ponder that, I'll invite you to another great birthday that I spend with God and Jesus Christ, and you can feel free to make it your own.

17

Another Great Birthday

As some of you know from reading "God's Cabin," the birthday I spent with God and Jesus Christ was by far the greatest birthday I ever had. This newer one will also be just as fabulous, but it will also have a very superior teachable moment.

I want you to know, however, I will be taking you to another special place as well as God's Cabin. It will be to an incredible canyon that I don't think more than fifty people know about. It's about a two-mile hike from God's Cabin, and I don't know of any road that goes to it. I came across it sort of by accident in my days of looking for quartz and other colors of stones. I shared my favorite rock with you in one of those chapters that lead to the greatest birthday gift of my life. What I didn't tell you about was my second favorite color of rock, which are red ones, maybe because I hardly ever find them. They are solid red and sometimes have streaks of white marble in them. In fact, Linda, who types my more current books, found a rather large spearhead made from a red rock, and it is priceless.

Anyway, I knew that I was gonna spend this birthday with God and Jesus starting out at the cross that sits just in front of God's cabin. Then I went right to this canyon. They both let me know in advance that it would be a truly spiritual day, and that it would be a birthday that I would always remember. They also told me to come back to their cross before I left that day because they had something to tell me, something for me to share with everyone I could. I gave them a more exuberant, greater glory for that, and I happily went to hike the canyon.

It's not a real easy walk because it takes a good half hour of going through the hot desert sand. There's also big rocks and some mighty big dips and dives. However, on the pathway I have made, suddenly I was finding a lot of red rocks that were never there before. I was so very happy, especially because I knew that God and Jesus were making this deliverance to be possible. I was finding so many in a variety of shapes and sizes and my five-gallon bucket was really getting heavy with them. Down in a gully, I found one that was so big, there was no way it would ever fit into the bucket. I left it alone and proceeded toward the canyon. I walked along the southern edge of it as I had a dozen or more times, walking in the same footsteps as before. I also kept on finding all these beautiful red rocks that I knew were never there in my previous visits to this canyon.

Then my eyes saw a shine from a different color that was about ten feet away. When I got up to it, I could see as plain as day that it was a stunning piece of petrified wood. I had never seen a piece of petrified wood with this color at all—not in stores or museums or in any person's collection. The color was a deep, shiny brown, and it looked like a big chunk of fresh chocolate. It was about as big as one of those large chocolate Easter bunny rabbits, and I was ecstatic. It was by far the best piece of petrified wood I have ever found, and it was a very great birthday gift from God and Jesus. With all the red rocks they had me find and now for this ultra-amazing piece of chocolate-colored petrified wood, I had a grin on me wider than this canyon.

I wanted to go down into the canyon, but I am not a "cliff climbing up or down" kind of a person. There is also a cougar down there. As I walk around the top, I see their tracks, so I am always on the lookout for them. I can even see where they might put their dens because of the rock formations and caves that are on both sides of this canyon. This canyon is so unique because God made lots of tractor-trailer-sized boulders in it. There are hundreds of boulders that make cars look like pebbles on the edges of this canyon. At the bottom of the canyon, there is a huge, deep gorge that I have yet to walk in. The gorge was formed by centuries of erosion that have eaten away at the canyon walls.

I mean, you have to see this canyon to believe how unique it really is. I think if you believe in God and Jesus Christ, then you will get a real good feel for it, just like you can for this extra glorious birthday that is not quite over yet. Please stay with me because if you do and try hard, then you might be able to hear the voice of God and Jesus.

Yes, I knew I had to go back to God's Cabin because they had told me they had something to tell me for something they wanted me to share with as many people as I could. I fully thanked them both before I left, and I sure gave them all of their more than well-deserved super glory. It felt so great to do that, and I felt bigger than all those massive, huge boulders all put together. Even my heart was feeling larger, my spirit for God and Jesus was accelerating, and even though I had no clue what they wanted to tell me at the cross, I knew that it would be important because everything they both ever say to me at their cross has always been revealing, transforming, and has always been teachable. All their other events at the cross have been made to be with us forever, and I knew that this would be another one of this caliber.

I then went up to the cross with my shirt off because I just had to wrap my bare arms and chest around it, so the feeling I have for Jesus would become forever penetrating. Yes, this was the way it had to be, and I knew that the heat of his blood would burn deep into every cell of my body. I thanked them again for such a very great birthday and for all their kind gifts. I then started praying that what they would say to me would be so uplifting and to be a spiritual guidance that nobody at all could ever dispute it and to be so revealing that it would easily make all our pathways to heaven become more certain.

I hugged their cross tighter and prayed for them to do what they have always done for a not-so-smart person like me, to just keep their words be so simple, right to the point where I could easily write them out so that anybody would be able to understand them. Here is exactly what they said: "*When we commit a sin, we actually sin twice.*" Now that you know, I will explain the other words of importance as our conversation continued.

The first sin is the sin in *itself,* and the second sin is always attached to the first sin, and it is caused by our being *selfish.* They firmly told me that when we make the sin itself, they always take full notice of it. This then takes precious time away from them because it also takes time for them to record it. In that second sin of selfishness, the time we take away from them could be the time that they could heal somebody, reach somebody, or teach somebody, save somebody's life, and the list of things that they could do for the better of all of us goes on and on. They both never ever miss out on anything that anybody does, and for us to *respect their time* is extremely important to them both. You can fight what they both told me to tell you all the way to the tops of God's canyons, but on the top of them all, they will always have the same one word. That word is *choice*.

I may not write out the words that you are reading to ever be at 1,000 percent perfect, but they are always a zillion percent honest. Their godly truth and doing all that we can to live to the very edge of perfection, for God and Jesus Christ is all about their very words, best intentions, simple learning of the true, spiritual commitment, praying, faith, hope, and a great desire to live for the great God and Jesus Christ's story. It is a most wonderful blessing to acquire; it is also a blessing to strive for. No, I am not perfect, none of us are, but all of us can let the blood of Jesus and the light of God mix in for our *acceleration*.

Therefore, when you think about all that has been written so far in this book or any of the others, I think that any rational person would easily agree that nobody has been asked to do anything that is really hard to do. *Choice* is a real easy word to figure out and *love*; after all, it has four simple letters. Full eternal love for God and Jesus Christ is absolutely possible, but you gotta want it.

God's Repair Shop and what it is asking is also not hard to interpret, but it does require people to fully understand the very next sentence; the best of all things that anybody can ever do is to do something for God and Jesus Christ, period. Yes, it's a matter of fact that once again brings us to the same very two questions. They are "Where are you spending your time, and who are you spending it with?" Two striking questions that always—yes, always—stay so relevant. As you give God and Jesus your best-spirited answers, I'll put the next chapter into its tasteful delight.

18

Banana

I may be the first person, or not, to title a chapter "Banana," but please know that God is always the first to make all great things whether it be the invention of the wheel, TV, or cell phones; but if God had not invented the *brain*, then nothing could ever have been invented at all.

Some of these inventions come to us by the blessings of God, and yes, even Jesus Christ has the power to always give us certain blessings every day, which could be a blessing to a single person or a bunch of people and even a country or countries. A fantastic blessing that God has delivered to the United States and some other places is the banana. You can laugh at that because it might sound silly, but if you live in America, then the opportunity to have a banana on any day of the year, in any season, God blesses us in America to have a banana or not. *They never run out.* They are extremely healthy, and I have never heard of anybody being allergic to them. I am sure that some people do not like them, but even they get a choice to think of how they feel about bananas.

So why do I bring this up? It is because the banana is so taken for granted. In America, God and Jesus Christ are also taken for granted by way to many people. It can be by those who believe in them both yet always think that the blessing of heaven is going to be automatic, especially if they truly believe in the phrase *"Once saved, always saved."* We sometimes hear of a person who is very mad at God and Jesus, and then, as they stay mad, they think a great blessing or a gift from them is going to be on their very doorstep. It even appears that our government is very convinced that the blessings to America will come forever automatically. Yet they flaunt with morality, death by abortion, massive ungodly debt, and when or if they mention God and Jesus Christ, it's usually so quick that it seems like an add-on. I really am not a smart person at all, but even I can figure out that nobody ever should take God and Jesus for granted, and neither should any country. I love America, I fought for its freedom to keep the integrity of the USA, but like so many I talk to, we know America is on a hateful, dividing slippery slope that God and Jesus have also noticed.

Let me give you an example of a name that is attached to a number: *COVID-19*. We have seen some of our government officials close many church doors because of it, try to force vaccines on people who have legitimate religious exemptions, and to take some of our freedoms away. It even appears that they, along with some of the media, want to instill the fear of God in us. However, if you have truly made God and Jesus Christ be your very best friends, then you do not have to hit the panic button on anything. It's true that COVID-19 has, by questionable government statistics, killed a lot of sick people, and it could even continue. However, the majority of them had other serious health issues. A lot smoked dangerous products, drank dangerous things, and many were obese or elderly with other diseases. These people would probably be lost soon because of their health problems, but to me, something else got very lost, such as the opportunity to instill healthy ways of living for us. To me, to be trained to wear a mask for so many hours of the day is a bad way to cut down on oxygen provided by God. Breathing trapped carbon dioxide, in my opinion, is not smart or healthy either. Some leaders also made mask mandates to hide your face from God and Jesus on any given day. *But take notice!* You almost never see a mask on the face of Dr. Fauci and other doctors on TV who always tell us that you just gotta wear a mask. Even many in the media who tell us the same thing show themselves to be mask-less. They will tell us they are not near anybody but shouldn't they wear a mask to set the example, or is talk cheap? Is their way of talking to be slippery just like a banana peel? After all, how often do they talk about or bring up God and Jesus Christ, especially because God and Jesus can heal and can save lives. They can also put an end to a pandemic because they, from their blessings, have given us ways to do this in the past with real God-given vaccines that don't require booster shot after booster shots.

This, to me, brings up the question of where do you put your faith? Who do you trust, and why does anybody want any person to hide their face from God and Jesus Christ? It is even written in godly words that I saw somewhere *that we with unveiled faces are being transformed into the image of God. How can God or Jesus transform a face that is in hiding?* Why don't others who should know this tell you that? Why did so many of them forget that America is or was supposed to have the church be separate from the government? Why did so many not protest about God's church doors being closed by overreaching mayors and governors? Did they not have trust in God and Jesus Christ? In fact, almost every church could have *kept their doors open* if they went to a seven-day-a-week schedule using an alphabetic letter system to be put in place with a social distancing seating arrangement.

It's not hard to figure something like that out, but the best way to learn anything comes from the direct wisdom and knowledge that God and Jesus both love to pass out to anybody who is receptive. It sort of coincides with wanting their blessings. To get blessed by God and Jesus Christ is available to every single person on this Earth, period. Their blessings are also available to every country, politician, and to all world leaders, but all of us together gotta want to be living for God and Jesus Christ.

Yes, blessings come in all shapes and sizes, and so many different kinds of butterfly colors that God and Jesus just love to pass out. They both even bless people who don't even realize that, even those who do not believe in that. Just ask yourself this easy question: Why are there always thousands if not millions of tons of bananas available to us 365 days a year?

Please give that question your best-thought-out, fruit-filled answer whether you believe in my two very most blessing friends or even if you do not. Take all the precious time you may need because I am going eat a blessed banana and slide right into the very next chapter.

19

The Story of Sol

This will be a true life-and-death story that God blessed me to be a verbal witness to. It will catch your attention, especially if you are married or if you just love somebody dearly. I was in the same senior trailer park at the time by Daytona Beach, Florida, and again cannot be specific on the date I used to walk or ride my bike to the clubhouse a lot because that's where my ninety-year-old friend, Bill, hung out.

This story is not about Bill, but I want you to know how awesome Bill was. He won almost every game of Scrabble he ever played, and he could do ten push-ups in front of anybody who thought that all of his physical capabilities were gone. He also did something else that I saw that was so remarkable. If he felt like having a store-bought sandwich, he would take a hold of his walker and then walk over a mile and a half to go get one. It was a three-mile round trip that I don't think a lot of out of shape people could accomplish on any given day.

However, this chapter's primary purpose is to give you a better-spirited feel for heaven. It's also about a very mellow elderly friend whose first name is Sol and his wife whom I never met. They lived year-round at this senior mobile home park where I spent about three months during the winter for a few years. Being new at this senior place, I met Sol at the clubhouse. We started talking, and I could instantly pick up that he was extremely genteel and stellar. He also told me that he was eighty years old, and that he and his wife were married for almost sixty years. When he mentioned his wife, his eyes got wet and a sad tear came out of one of them. I immediately knew that something was wrong, and Sol was hurting. I didn't press it, but as the conversation continued, another tear came out. He then mentioned his wife again and said his wife had an incurable cancer. Sol then left the clubhouse because he had to tend to his dying wife. After my first conversation with Sol, I would see him at the clubhouse about once a week. I would always comfort Sol when his wife came up in the conversation, and in one of those early conversations, I gave him a photo of the crown of Jesus.

Sol had already told me that he and his wife were true, full-faith believers in God and Jesus Christ They both also knew that she would be going to heaven. It's a certain feeling that is entirely possible, especially to those who live inside of *the real godly truth*. Sol, in our conversations, also told me how much his wife had loved making craft items and how she loved teaching other people to make them. He also told me that in moving to different places during their marriage, how his wife volunteered to form and lead an array of different craft clubs. In fact, she was in charge of the one at this senior park until she became bedridden from her cancer. I could see the pride in his eyes when he said that. Then Sol told me that both he and his wife volunteered to help others many times before, and for many, many years. It's called the *joy of serving*, in case anybody is interested, and it can start with a little thing like becoming polite to people instead of a "road-rage" attitude.

Yes, the joy of serving is a great way to live for God and Jesus and for people, especially if you expect nothing in return. I am not an expert about it either, but surely, they want me to say this once again. Nobody will ever be able to do anything better than doing something for God and Jesus Christ. Serving them both, serving other people in one way or another or in several other ways will warm you up way more than a hot July desert sun, that's for sure. So why not try it so that you can measure the feel-good results.

Serving others, in fact, has some other big advantages also. It can reduce stress, reduce anger, and even eliminate them, and it even has a way to eliminate hatred. The list can be added to but a person has to simply figure it out. You can also call on God and Jesus Christ because they will be more than glad to help anybody with this.

But you just gotta ask them just like Sol was asking for comfort and to understand his wife's dying from a deadly cancer. *God and Jesus Christ delivered.* They were spiritually helping him through this terrible time in his life, and Sol did not get angry at them. Sol understood this death to be an eternal life transition. Sol prayed in earnest and drew strength from the photo of the crown of Jesus, from other comforting people and a certain strength directly from God and Jesus Christ themselves. It is a certain strength that is mostly reserved for those who really know God and Jesus or at least want to.

However, like most people, Sol had a very specific question to ask his dying wife, and it was not "Why are you leaving me?" No, his question was quite different, but in all their glory, both God and Jesus gave his wife the right and most sincere words to say to him when he gently ask her the following question: "Where will I find you when I get to heaven so that I can be with you forever?"

She just smiled as she placed his head toward her lips and softly said, "*You can find me at the craft shop* because Jesus has told me that's where I will be."

Sol told me this after his wife had passed, and the pride in his eyes shined like asteroids making a night sky look like daylight. You see, both God and Jesus Christ have the ability and exclusive power to get their messages out in any way they want to. But you sure gotta believe in them and listen with passion to all of their graceful words. They both always want to share themselves with all of you, but you just have to want to share yourself with them. The popcorn lady, Sol and his wife clearly understood the power of listening, the power of serving, and so much more about God and Jesus Christ. The popcorn lady and Sol's dying wife knew in advance not only their destiny to heaven, but exactly where they would be inside of it. They even knew the exact thing of what they would be doing in heaven.

Now you don't have to believe that but both God and Jesus have more than proven themselves over and over. Proving that they are more than happy to bless us with our *heart's desires*, especially if it is the will of God. Having people know in advance what they will be doing in heaven or where they will be in heaven is minuscule for both of them, especially because they can give us full eternal real life after death.

They may not do this for everybody because way too many people don't give them a lot of meaningful time in the day or no time at all. A lot of people have heard of God and Jesus Christ, but that is minuscule to really knowing them both. Very few people pray for God and Jesus Christ *first* on a daily basis or never pray for them at all. Sadly, a lot of people pray for themselves first with a "me first and only" attitude even if they go to church for an hour each week. This may satisfy a "first base" only feeling but I, as a nonsmart, non-preacher person would suggest that everybody get themselves to home plate, standing up instead of trying to somehow slide in.

It is or can be a base-by-base process because I know from my own experience that it took me right around seventy years to have a full victory at home plate with God and Jesus Christ. That's way too many lost years for anybody, but regardless of whether you are younger or older, you can surely have the full Jesus Christ blood in your home-plate victory with my two best friends as the super radiant light of God flashes on the scoreboard.

In fact, anybody can have expedited, exceptional victories many times over with God and Jesus Christ just like Sol, the popcorn lady, and the many butterflies did. Whenever you serve somebody or lots of people and then expect nothing in return, the victories can really build up. I could even go on and on with this, but I'd rather share a two-times story with all of you in the next heaven-bound chapter. So please take a deep, refreshing breath and open your eyes as wide a possible so you get a better insight into heaven.

20

Two Times to Heaven

In my first book, *A Crown for Jesus*, they both had me write out for you that in a future book I would share the stories of the two times they took me to heaven. It would have been convenient to write it out back then, but God and Jesus do not always go by what is convenient for me, you, or anybody else. No, they have their own way and plan, and this is always in their timing. The only thing anybody can do to *speed* some things up for the purposes of God and Jesus Christ is to become their very best committed friends *sooner* rather than later. I could elaborate on this more, but I know that they will both appreciate anybody's effort to carry this out further on their own.

Therefore, I'll get to those two times to heaven, but first, I want you to know the following. These two times happened within a year of them making the crown of Jesus in the sky and their first special, all-exciting rainbow in 2013. I can't give you the specific dates for either of these heaven events or the exact time of my being taken there or when my feet touched the Earth again. I can tell you as I'm writing this that they have not taken me back there since the last time, but after what I saw and know, going back there for all eternity is gonna be way, way better than all of the nicest, greatest dreams of all of us put together have ever had or can ever have. I also want you to know that they did not show me all of heaven. However, from what they showed me the first time, they make it way more than obvious that heaven never ever ends. Soon, you will understand and appreciate that.

I also did not see anybody there nor any angels because it was by them both for me not to see them. I also did not see God or Jesus

Christ but their spirit flew way, way stronger than all of the water that drops down from all the waterfalls on this Earth and all the waves that all of oceans worldwide smash down with.

In either trip, I never got scared or even thought about it, and believe it or not, I never had any "fireworks" excitement. That's because what overtook me in heaven was the *pure peace* of godly calmness. I was in such awe to what I was seeing because, in all honesty, there is nothing on Earth to compare to its glorious vividness. Each of the two places, however, had their own dramatic realities and each of the two places had its certain reasons for why I was taken there. I also want you to especially know that understanding them will be simple because to date, absolutely everything that God and Jesus brings me or to have me experience is never complicated at all, which shows us just how glorious they both really are.

I will share the first place they took me. I was just standing in the yard of my home in South Carolina in the daylight, and I was put in a sort of unconscious state—not completely, though, because I could feel a definite movement. It was sort of like a transition that I could easily feel happening. In those first few minutes, I did not know where I was. Then the most extraordinary feeling of peace totally took me over and my vision could clearly see far beyond any distance I had ever taken notice of. I then looked from side to side, and although I did not see anything that stood out in particular, there was one thing that I truly focused on. It was the *peace*. It was way more than just a feeling of fantastic, easy goodness, but it was so great that I could touch it and taste it. Yes, it was everywhere, and I really do have to apologize because in whatever time I have left here on God's Earth, I will never be able to write the special words to describe this pure and clean God-given, ultra, amazing peace.

I was standing, looking from side to side in this peace, and I was so taken by its glamour that I never even looked behind me to see more of God's heaven that I knew was there. I looked forward again, and then God did something so spectacular for us. He made a huge silver ball far bigger than the moon, and it shined far greater than all of the brightest chrome in all the world. Greater than all the brightest chrome on every Harley Davidson and all the chrome that reflects at the worldwide car shows. They could never come close to this chrome ball at all. I was breathing, but in a way, I was breathless because I knew for sure that I was now in heaven and only God's heaven could ever have this. I was concentrating on this chrome ball so much, but then God asked me softly but firmly this question: "Would you like me to make a ball out of gold?" Without even thinking about it, I just said no. Then I said, "Not really because gold is of no interest to me, and I don't have any to speak of."

Then God asked me this: "Would you like to see me make a diamond this big or even bigger?" Again, I said no because in God's truth, diamonds are not important to me. Then God said, "Would you like me to make mountains of jewelry for you?"

Again, I said "no." I then said, "Lord, no, that's okay because I don't have any jewelry, and I am just not interested in it at all."

God then said, "I know that because I do know what your *heart truly desires* beside me and my Son." I just smiled at that, and instantly the peace got even better. Suddenly, another huge silver ball appeared, then another, and one after another, and they kept on quickly appearing by multiple thousands. In fact, I don't even think that a high-speed calculator could have kept up with counting them. You see, God was creating a new heavenly universe of silver chrome balls in front of me as he was letting me know the following, that he and Jesus Christ have all *the power, all authority*, and soon they will have the only kingdom on this Earth. The message was way more than silver-chrome clear. I was then placed back at my home in South Carolina, and I was so ecstatic for that experience.

Yet I knew that God wanted me to be reserved and for me to keep this heavenly description from being written out until they wanted it released, and this would come by the true grace of their own timing. They will, in fact, give all of you a choice to believe in this or not. So please let me ask you this: what do you have to believe in that's better than God and Jesus Christ or better than this heavenly experience? What do any of you have that's far more convincing than the evidence that God and Jesus Christ gave to us by them making the very crown of Jesus in the sky in March of 2013? I mean, every day in the world both God and Jesus just keep on producing evidence from their blessings to us by them or events by them from other people's photographs that they allow and so much more.

Yes, they both have a history of sensational righteousness, and that's why Hitler and his henchmen lost the second world war. That's also why, about thirty years ago, the unranked USA amateur hockey team beat the ultra, super-professional Russian hockey team and went on to win it all. Putin and the other world leaders might stay in a state of denial, but the godly truth is *all of the greatest things happen* only because of the amazing power of God and Jesus Christ. Yes, there are certainly trials and hard or extremely difficult times, maybe even worse than that, but the real truth is this: nobody will know what real godly joy is unless they get to experience an opposite emotional feeling. If you can understand that, then this second time to heaven event will have a very special meaning and applying it to yourself will be possible. All of you can own it and place this somewhere inside of your other heavenly God and Jesus Christ stories.

With that purposely said, I was just sitting inside my South Carolina home and again felt this slight drifting away. I then felt an upward movement, and soon I found myself standing in a paradise that had *heaven* written all over it. Suddenly, my eyes saw a most beautiful grassy area about an acre in size. This grass was not the grass on Earth in any way at all. It's color of green was so majestic, and it looked as soft as the most gentle, puffy cloud ever made. I then saw a beautiful pond that was instantly made that was placed in front of the grass. It was also a thousand times cleaner than a brand-new mirror that came out of its wrapping. I was taken in by it for several minutes, and then I looked at the vegetation and all the trees that were in the surrounding areas. They were virgin, and every feature they had dazzled in a most shimmering, distinctive elegance. I then saw a pathway that came to the grass from the distance and then looked at the softest beautiful grass again that God could ever make. I got very emotional from looking at it because at a zillion percent, I knew that God and Jesus had made it for me. Yes, I got this most sensational relief from a super godly great spirit, and I got so fantastically happy, that's for sure.

Then, just like that, God said to me, *"I know that this is what your heart desires and what you have asked for."*

I said, "Yes, it sure is, and it's even way better than I have prayed for. I have asked the both of you for most of my life ever since I got back from Vietnam."

God said, "We know that and we have prepared this place for you when you are here permanently."

I just had to thank them so very much as I gave them both all the ultra glory, but I also had to ask God this question: "What is the pathway for as I have never asked for that?" I could feel God smile as he then said, "That will take you to many other places in heaven when you want to go to them. Also, others may take this path to come and see you, especially those who have passed away and have meant so much to you." I could only say that I understood, but I could also instantly feel the people who had passed away that I had spent significant, meaningful, or emotional time with. I was then placed back in the room that I had left.

You see, both God and Jesus Christ had actually taken me to heaven these two times to benefit all of us. Let me explain: The *first time* God clearly showed us that he and Jesus have *all* of the power and every kind of authority. God also showed us that he alone is the master creator. Not only did he create the Earth that he has gifted to us but also every square inch of the universe and his place called heaven. Heaven is really a never-ending place, and he showcased it by adding a bigger than the moon silver chrome ball right in front of my eyes and then so many more that nobody will ever be able to count them as they reach out to extend heaven a lot further. God and Jesus even tested me after the first silver chrome ball was made by asking me directly if I wanted to see one made of gold or of a diamond and also a mountain range of jewelry.

I said no to all of those, and they then knew at a zillion percent that it truly was forever in me to want to be a very best committed, desiring friend of theirs. This also let them clearly know that they were who I wanted to spend my time with and where I wanted to spend it for all eternity. I could expand on that further, but there is a Bible to guide anybody who has a desiring quest for God and Jesus Christ. There's also many preachers, teachers, and others, books of all kinds, and yes, even the four previous books that God and Jesus had me experience. Those books are simple to read, and all of them have all the grace of God and Jesus Christ from cover to cover. They are also written so that anybody can place themselves into the God and Jesus Christ stories.

In fact, that's what God and Jesus demonstrated to us when they took me to a special part of heaven the second time. It proves to everybody that they both can easily give to any person what their heart truly desires if it is within their will. Remember, however, that they absolutely tested me in the first trip to heaven, and if I had failed by greed, lust, or something else, they have no use for, then the second time would have not happened at all. A rather very simple conclusion because they both will always test our inner heart's sincerity.

I can't say what you or anybody else truly desires more than anything else, but I will at least make a recommendation: any heart's desire should always be about God and Jesus Christ exclusively. I could even go on and on with this, but if you got to this place, then in my heart, I have to believe that you simply have a lot of God and Jesus Christ on your mind. Having a great relationship with both of them is in anybody's favor by having them become your best friends for the first time, but you gotta want them more than anything else.

God and Jesus are kind and gentle, and they are so very understanding. They are also very *forgiving*, especially if your heart is in the right place of real sincerity. They have even blessed us with other telling examples such as the popcorn lady, Sol and his craft-loving wife, and the woman who was woken up by mega billions of beautiful butterflies. There are also millions upon millions of other God and Jesus real knowing people, and many have other real great godly truth stories. Finding at least one certain Jesus Christ story is there to be had, but you just have to do some seeking in faith of believing.

Yes, there really are super great stories about God and his mighty son Jesus everywhere, and if you have gotten this far, then I feel that all of you are more than entitled to have this last, ending story to be put into your memory bank. It will show all of you that both God and Jesus Christ are way quicker than lightning and how they both step into a situation to help you get out of a jam. Because I think all of you will appreciate it, I will place it in a chapter of its own.

21

Lake Trash

This took place in Florida at the senior trailer park where I would spend a couple of months in the winter. I have to give you some of the groundwork first that goes along with this story's creation. Then I'll write out the story's substance. Its location was at the clubhouse of this trailer park where I was blessed to hang out with Bill and a couple of other friends who were connected to God and Jesus. There was also another man who hung out there named George. He is a full-time laptop user and a zillion percent atheist. To me, he lived for two specific reasons of which I had no interest in. One was the stock market. I'll admit, he was very good in making money this way. The other was using a lot of his time by focusing in finding out lots of things on his laptop computer. He would also listen to conversations around him, and then would look up what was said on his laptop, just hoping he could catch somebody in a lie.

I didn't really care about that so much, and as some of you know already, I have absolutely no interest in computers, smartphones, or anything like that at all. In God's truth, I have no idea what an e-mail looks like, and I have no way to receive one or send one out. I have never used an ATM or a debit card either, and I really like my VCR. Not that those things are a big part of this story, but in a way, they sort of are. You see, when you never use these things, they are hardly, if ever, on your mind.

One day, I was at a thrift store, and they had a brand-new hat that boldly said *"Lake Trash."* I mean, you could never miss it because the hat was bright, jet-black, and had the words "Lake Trash" embossed in big extra bright gold letters. I bought it for a dollar and started wearing it when I went somewhere. This let me to frequently be asked, "*Where's Lake Trash?*" I had no idea where it was, and in fact, I had no idea if there was any lake that was named "Lake Trash." I took it upon myself to just jokingly answer this question by saying either in New York or in Texas. After all, these were two huge states, and I was very confident that it would never be disputed. Well, anyway, after a couple of weeks wearing this hat almost everywhere, I decided to wear it the clubhouse and "laptop" George was there. He saw my Lake Trash hat on my head, and sure enough, he asked me, "Where's Trash Lake?"

For some reason, I quickly blurted out "Montana" and then sat down about twenty feet away from him with two of my good Christian friends. They smiled at my hat and had heard atheist George ask me where Lake Trash was. Yes, George asked me that loudly and then got right to his laptop. I said to my two friends that I had no idea where it was, and I had just made that up for George. Suddenly, George shouted out, "Hey, Lance! You're right. Here it is. *It's right here in Montana* just like you said it was." He then said, "Come and look on my computer so I can show it to you." I walked over to see it in a sort of relieved way because in God's truth, I had absolutely no idea where Lake Trash was when I said Montana to George. I even thought to myself, *How could I ever have come up with that?*

Before my next step, I knew the very reason because I could feel the presence of God and Jesus wink at me. Yes, they captured the moment and saved my day, for sure. I was so extra happy and I could absolutely feel the ultra happiness of God and Jesus Christ to be with me. They were both not only with me for this one time, but also for so many, many times before. They even are with anybody who wants to be with them and even with those who do not want to be with them at all. They both truly want to become a very special part of everybody's story, and they surely always do this by giving all of us a simple work called *choice.*

With that said, one of my forever prayers will always be for everybody on this Earth to make a choice to become the best of forever friends with God and Jesus Christ.

A Personal Message

Thanks so much for the certain time you just gave to God and Jesus Christ. I pray that a lot of your present and future time will be spent in earnest with both of them. We (God, Jesus, and I) hope you all understood and appreciated those two heavenly places that were presented to you so that your faith and confidence in God and Jesus Christ grow far beyond the farthest silver chrome ball. They are there to be seen if you will let them become a part of your heart's desire. We pray in the word of *serving* and word of *choice*. We hope all of you will always give your vote to God and Jesus Christ on an everyday basis because they do *vote* for us every day. Always remember to give them both their well-deserved glory and always allow yourselves to become a significant part of their most glorious stories.

Sincerely,
Lance Tassi

The next book shall be titled *The Death of Rose* or *The Choice of Heaven or Hell*.

The first four books are titled in order:

1. *A Crown for Jesus*
2. *A Perfect Peace*
3. *God's Cabin*
4. *The Godly Truth*

All of them are currently available and are published by Christian Faith Publishing.

Acknowledgments

I would forever like to thank God and Jesus Christ for all these important stories that they have presented to me so that we could present all of them to you, thus confirming that it is only by Them who can make all things to be possible.

I would like to thank Kathy Winfree for typing my first two books and for all the other things she keeps doing to help bring these many words from God and Jesus to you. She and her husband have also taken their ministries far beyond the shores of America.

I would also like to thank Linda McMahill for typing the last three books, one of them which is now in your possession. Her encouragement is a truly divine blessing. You should also know for the past ten years in a row, she has read the Bible from cover to cover. Linda, truly, is a full-faith believer in God and Jesus Christ. She has also been to the *doorstep* of God's Cabin and is living proof that God and Jesus can truly make a way for anybody who thinks there is no way at all.

So please thank all of them for their help in bringing more of God and Jesus Christ to all of you.

About the Author

Lance Tassi brings to all of you the events, findings stories, photographs, and the conversations that he had with God and Jesus.

It is from the three of them to use these revelations for the divine purpose of *moving* the crown of Jesus Christ forward.

All of you are more than invited to join them.